BREEDERS' BE

A KENNEL CLUB B

Pomeranian

By Olga Baker

BREEDERS' BEST™

A KENNEL CLUB BOOK®

POMERANIAN

ISBN: 1-59378-911-4

Copyright © 2005

Kennel Club Books, LLC
308 Main Street, Allenhurst, NJ 07711 USA
Printed in South Korea

PHOTOS BY:
Ashbey Photography,
Paulette Braun, Isabelle Francais,
Dee and Bill Francis,
Carol Ann Johnson, Phoebe,
Karen Taylor and Connie Zieba

DRAWINGS BY:
Yolyanko el Habanero

Contents

Meet the Pomeranian

The Pomeranian is fondly known as the "Pom" and is a bouncy little dog that is absolutely full of fun and mischief. This is an intelligent, lively and beautiful toy breed whose compact size and remarkable good looks have made it an international favorite at dog shows, in homes in the city and country and in the pages of fashion magazines. The Pom we know today is much smaller than it was in years gone by, so don't be surprised if you see a 200-year-old painting of a

The compact size, beautiful coat and sparkling personality, evidenced by the grins on these playful Poms, are all part of the breed's undeniable appeal.

pretty darn big Pom-like dog sitting beside an elegant lady. The most famous example that comes to mind is Sir Thomas Gainsborough's portrait of the actress Mrs. Robinson with her Pomeranian. The breed then was in fact closer to the German Spitz, a breed that can still be found in Europe. In fact, most European countries today refer to the Pomeranian as the Toy German Spitz or *Deutscher Zwergspitz*. Indeed, some early representatives of the breed weighed as much as 50 pounds, far removed from the diminutive breed with which we are familiar now.

A Pomeranian in full show coat cuts quite a striking silhouette.

The name we Americans use for the breed comes from the breed's homeland of Pomerania, which used to be a duchy located between eastern Germany and western Poland. Although prized as ladies' pets in early Greece and Rome, the Pomeranian is actually a descendant of European

He doesn't come down the chimney, but a Pomeranian has many wonderful gifts to share with his family just the same.

working dogs. The breed is full of surprises, and the fact that in classical Greece it was called the "Maltese Dog" has been the cause of some confusion in the past.

The name "Pomeranian" seems to have first been recorded in 1792, when George Vancouver wrote of visiting a village in India where he came across dogs that resembled those of Pomerania, although they were larger in size. Very likely these dogs in India may have been the fairly common spitz-like dog that is still found there and is frequently called simply "the prick-eared dog."

Dogs of the same general type as today's Pomeranian, though larger, were known as the Wolfspitz, Fox-dog, Spitz-dog and Loup-Loup. They protected flocks of sheep and cattle from the wolf, reputedly with unfailing success. They were also used to control sheep and cattle and to round up reindeer. These early spitz dogs lie in the ancestry of many similar breeds known today, among them not only the Pom but also the American Eskimo Dog, Keeshond, Schipperke, Norwegian Elkhound and Samoyed.

In the wastelands of Russia and Siberia, the forerunner of today's Pom pulled sledges, and even the Russian Laika that was used in early space travel has a very similar ancestry to our tiny little friend.

England's King George III took as his wife Queen Charlotte, a noblewoman of German descent who favored the dogs of Pomerania. In 1767, she brought a pair of Pomeranians with her to Britain; these dogs were perpetuated on canvas. By 1870, the English Kennel Club had recognized the breed, then by the name of "Spitzdog," and when Queen Victoria, British queen of German descent (through the House of Hanover), took a fancy to the breed, public interest grew.

Queen Victoria was actually Queen Charlotte's granddaughter, but their blood connections have no bearing some of her dogs and, on occasion, even had a special class put on for her because she wished to exhibit a color not usually shown in England.

Members of British royalty favored this small spitz, spotlighting the Pom in the public eye.

on their common interest in the Pomeranian, as far as we know. Queen Victoria first encountered the breed in Italy in 1888, subsequently obtaining several dogs from Florence. Marco was the queen's much-adored red sable Pom; at a plump 12 pounds, he was considered a "valuable tiny Pomeranian"!

The queen actually showed For a while, the breed was even called the Victorian Pom! So highly sought after was the breed in Britain that, by the close of that century, Poms were selling for as much as £250. This meant that, ounce for pound, they were very probably the most expensive breed in any kingdom.

By the turn of the 20th century, the Pomeranian had

changed dramatically. The breed was smaller and more elegant. No longer was it looking after cattle and sheep or pulling sledges; instead, it had entered fashionable circles and weighed only around 6 pounds. The Pomeranian had become a Lilliputian, addicted to the laps of lovely ladies! Its very character had changed, so that it no longer had the reputation of being "snappish and untrustworthy." The breed had become affectionate, gentle and well behaved. In every way, the Pomeranian had become "a pattern for pet dogs."

The breed's colors were highly attractive, and different countries began to specialize in different colors. White Poms were found in France and red ones in Italy, and although there were black-and-white ones in the 19th century, they were not generally very good examples of the breed. Creams and reds were the most popular. By the 1880s, Britain had primarily white Poms. In about 1860, we know that there was a strain of rich fawns in the Midlands. Britain's first orange arrived on the scene in 1911, but not until the 1930s did a wide range of colors appear.

In the US, the year 1888 was significant in the breed's history, for this was when the first Pomeranian was recorded by the American Kennel Club (AKC). The breed was recognized in the US in 1900; by 1909, the American Pomeranian Club was accepted as a member of the AKC and became the official parent club of the breed. The breed's first specialty show took place the following year, with an entry of 138. The Best of Breed winner, a black dog, was named Ch. Canner Prince Charming. (Isn't that a great name for a Pom?)

It is not surprising that the Pom became a favorite in 1930s' America: the ever-happy, daffy Pom was the perfect antidote to the Depression! Throughout that dreary decade, show entries grew and many notable breeding lines were developed. Orange has long been the favored color in America, though different colors eventually came to the fore. A black Pom won a Best in Show award in the 1970s. In the early 1980s, we saw the first blue champion, followed shortly by the first chocolate champion. The first brindle-colored Pom had to wait to be crowned until as late as 1996, and the first blue sable became titled in 2003.

The author and her husband Darrell Baker have been "in Poms" since the 1970s. We actually started in Smooth Dachshunds! We attribute our first big winner to beginner's luck: Ch. Corn's Duke Dragonfly came in our second generation of Poms and proved to be a magnif-icent top winner and top producer. Since the days of

Duke, our Jeribeth Poms have had numerous champions, including some notable Best in Show winners.

Not the least of those wins was a momentous event in the history of the American Pomeranian (and one of the author's most cherished memories), which occurred on February 9, 1988, when Ch. Great Elms Prince Charming (a

Many Poms are kept as pampered pets, but, not surprisingly, the breed is also a favorite in the show ring worldwide.

CHAPTER 1

A historical win for the breed was Ch. Great Elms Prince Charming's Best in Show victory at Westminster in 1988. "Prince," co-owned by author Olga Baker and his handler Skip Piazza is the only Pom to have achieved this lofty victory. The judge on this great occasion was Michelle Billings.

BEST IN
SHOW

WESTMINSTER
KENNEL CLUB
FEB
1988

4.5-lb bright orange dog) won Best in Show at the prestigious Westminster Kennel Club Show in New York. The author co-owned Prince with his handler Skip Piazza, a darling friend who is much missed to this day. Prince was bred by Ruth Beam and was the first (and, to date, only) Pom ever to win at Westminster.

American Poms have also won top awards in obedience trials, and many have earned Canine Good Citizen® awards. Though a tiny breed, the Pom has also held its own in agility competition, and we're expecting great things in the rally obedience ring as well. The Pom continues to rank as one of America's top toy breeds in terms of AKC registrations among all breeds. It is clear to see how much the Pomeranian has found its way into the hearts of Americans from New York to California, Maine to Florida and, of course, Texas!

MEET THE POMERANIAN

Overview

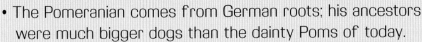

- The Pomeranian comes from German roots; his ancestors were much bigger dogs than the dainty Poms of today.
- The Pomeranian's ancestors were typically working dogs, serving as flock guardians, herding dogs and sledge-pullers.
- The Pom changed drastically during the 19th century; his size decreased and his temperament greatly improved. He became known as the favorite of British royalty and loved by the ladies as a lap dog.
- The Pom established a foothold in the US at the turn of the 20th century and his popularity here has never waned. He is one of the country's top toys in both the show ring and pet homes.

Description of the Pomeranian

An extroverted personality in a small package, the Pomeranian is great as a companion as well as a show dog. He is intelligent and vivacious, is sound and yet dainty, making this an appealing and much-loved breed. Let's take a look at the overall description of the ideal Pom, based on the AKC's standard for the breed. For all of his big-dog demeanor, there is no disputing the fact that a Pomeranian is a toy breed, weighing in, as he does, at only around 3 to 7 pounds, with the ideal

The Pom is a beautiful, sweet, lively dog and, best of all, the perfect size for picking up and cuddling, as Dorothy Nickles does with one of the author's Poms.

weight for a show dog being from 4 to 6 pounds. Although dog-show judges object to representatives over 7 pounds, overall quality and type are favored over size, especially where a healthy pet is concerned. The Pom is one of the few breeds in which the bitches tend to be larger than the males.

Grooming a Pom to look his impressive show-ring best is certainly something to smile about!

This is a short-backed active dog whose leg length is in proportion to a well-balanced frame. The distance from point of shoulder to point of buttocks is slightly shorter than from withers to ground and, to put this all into perspective, the distance from brisket to ground is about half the height at withers.

Despite his dainty appearance, the Pom is hearty and strong, and he is medium-boned. This is a cocky little breed, commanding in many ways and animated as he strides proudly around your living room, your back yard or the show ring. The Pom's

The Pomeranian draws large entries and crowds of spectators at shows. The Pom is also a popular choice for those who show dogs, as the breed's looks and personality make it a natural showstopper.

gait is smooth, free, balanced and vigorous. Neither front nor rear legs should be thrown out on the move; instead, the feet keep directly to the front so that movement is true. The topline should remain level, neither roached nor dipping.

The Pomeranian's head is in balance with the body, the muzzle rather short and free of lippiness. It should never be snipy. Sometimes a Pom can be found to have one or more molera, or holes, in the skull. This seems to happen especially in small specimens, but most molera close by about one year of age. The American Kennel Club breed standard states that the skull is to be closed and the top of the skull is required to be "slightly rounded, but not domed." The British standard states it should be "slightly" flat and "large in proportion to muzzle." In order to visualize the typical wedge shape of the head, you should imagine a line from the tips of the nose, ascending through the center of the eyes and the tip of the ears, which are small, mounted high and carried erect.

The Pom's alert expression is often described as "foxy," enhanced by dark, bright eyes that are medium-sized and almond- or oval-shaped. Let me clarify here that the term "foxy" does not mean "looking like a fox," but rather it describes the expression not the head shape. The eyes are "set well into the skull." The stop is well-pronounced. Pigmentation of the nose and eye rims is black in white, orange and shaded-sable dogs; brown in self-colored dogs (such as chocolate-tipped

The Keeshond is one of the Pom's close relatives, on the larger end of the German Spitz spectrum.

sable, brown, beaver and blue dogs). The nose should never be parti-colored or flesh-colored. White, orange, shaded-sable and cream dogs have black eye rims.

Teeth in toy breeds can be problematic, and the Pom is no exception to this rule. Young Poms usually have strong white teeth that meet in a scissors bite, which is the correct bite for the Pom, though tooth loss is common in the breed, even at a young age. Puppy teeth are as sharp as needles, and new owners learn this very quickly. These tiny teeth can clasp onto your fingers or toes and you will know it. There's nothing cute about this. Fortunately, the adult teeth emerge at around six months of age; less sharp, the adult teeth will hopefully not be grabbing onto your fingers once you have trained the puppy to behave.

The head is set onto a short neck, its base well set into the shoulders, which are suffi-ciently laid back for a high, proud carriage of the neck and head. The Pom's shoulder blade and the upper arm are equal in length, and both shoulders and legs should be moderately well muscled. With a short back and level topline, the Pom is a compact dog, well

The Pom derived from the larger German Spitz, who shares the typical spitz traits, among them small prick ears, short pointed muzzle, abundant coat and well-furred tail that lies over the back.

ribbed and with the brisket reaching below the elbow. The forelegs are straight and parallel to each other; the straight, strong pasterns lead to well-arched, compact feet that turn neither in nor out.

The hindquarters balance with the forequarters in angulation, and the buttocks

Occiput: Upper back part of skull; apex.

Skull: Cranium.

Stop: Indentation between eyes at point of nasal bones and skull.

Muzzle: Foreface or region of head in front of eyes.

Lips: Fleshy portion of upper and lower jaws.

Withers: Highest part of back, at base of neck above shoulders.

Shoulder: Upper point of forequarters; region of the two shoulder blades.

Forechest: Sternum.

Chest: Thoracic cavity (enclosed by ribs).

Forequarters: Front assembly from shoulder to feet.

Upper arm: Region between shoulder blade and elbow.

Forearm: Region between elbow and wrist.

Elbow: Region where upper arm and forearm meet.

Carpus: Wrist.

Brisket: Lower chest.

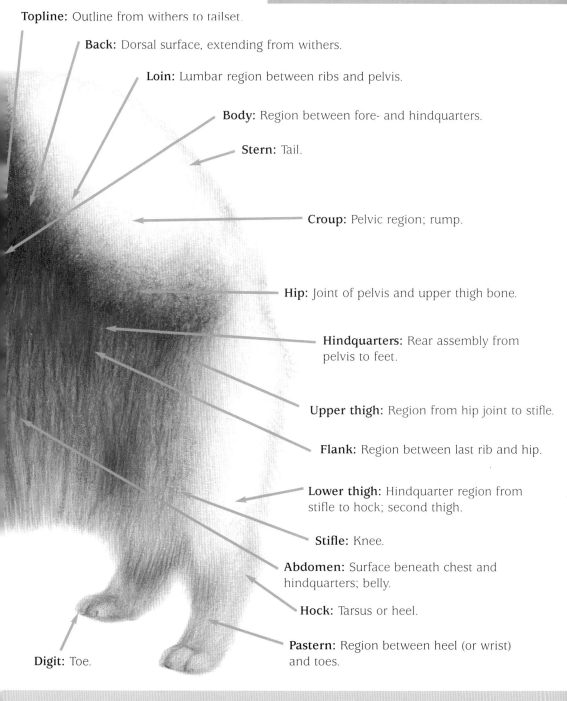

Topline: Outline from withers to tailset.

Back: Dorsal surface, extending from withers.

Loin: Lumbar region between ribs and pelvis.

Body: Region between fore- and hindquarters.

Stern: Tail.

Croup: Pelvic region; rump.

Hip: Joint of pelvis and upper thigh bone.

Hindquarters: Rear assembly from pelvis to feet.

Upper thigh: Region from hip joint to stifle.

Flank: Region between last rib and hip.

Lower thigh: Hindquarter region from stifle to hock; second thigh.

Stifle: Knee.

Abdomen: Surface beneath chest and hindquarters; belly.

Hock: Tarsus or heel.

Pastern: Region between heel (or wrist) and toes.

Digit: Toe.

are well behind the set of the tail. "Moderate" best describes the hindquarters: the thighs moderately muscled and the stifles, which are clearly defined, moderately bent. Hindlegs, too, are straight and parallel to each other, the feet well arched, compact and facing forward, like the front feet. The Pom stands well up on his toes.

The Pom's gait is described in the AKC standard as "smooth, free, balanced and vigorous." On the move, a Pom has good reach in the forequarters and good drive from behind, the hindlegs moving in line with the front legs. In order to achieve balance, the legs will converge slightly inward toward a center line when the dog is moving, but the legs should not be thrown in or out.

Noted for his beautiful double coat, the Pomeranian has a soft, dense undercoat with a long, straight, harsh-textured outer coat. The thickness of the undercoat allows the guard hair to "stand off" from the body. The coat is particularly profuse around the neck, the front of the shoulders and the chest; this hair forms the Pom's characteristic "frill" around the shoulders and chest. Forequarters are "well feathered to the hock," and the tail is covered with "long, harsh, spreading straight hair." On the head and legs, the coat is dense and shorter in length than the body coat. Indeed, perhaps the Pomeranian's crowning glory is the breed's characteristic beautifully plumed tail, which lies flat and straight on the back.

In the show ring, the Pomeranian's coat is his defining feature. The coat must not be soft, flat or sparsely haired, off-standing or lacking in undercoat. Trimming is allowed to give a clean, neat outline.

Finally, we come to color.

Although some people may have a personal preference, all colors, patterns and variations are allowed and judged equally in the show ring. There can be no mistaking that the Pomeranian is as colorful as a breed can be. The American Kennel Club standard is very specific about color-pattern definition: "Patterns: Black and Tan—tan or rust sharply defined, appearing above each eye and on muzzle, throat and forechest, on all legs and feet and below the tail. The richer the tan the more desirable; Brindle—the base color is gold, red or orange-brindled with strong black cross stripes; Parti-color—is white with any other color distributed in patches with a white blaze preferred on the head." The standard then goes on to identify color divisions that may be implemented at breed shows.

DESCRIPTION OF THE POMERANIAN

Overview

- A description that sums it up is that the Pomeranian is a big personality in a dainty little package. This is a tiny yet hearty and vivacious breed.
- The Pom has a wedge-shaped head, carried proudly, with small prick ears, dark pigmentation and a typically "foxy" expression.
- The Pomeranian is both small and compact, with a short back, balanced angulation and strong, straight legs.
- The Pom's double coat is his signature feature. With a dense coat all over the body, and the regal frill and plumed tail, the Pom's coat in correct condition is a magnificent sight.
- The breed's beautiful coat can be seen in a rainbow of colors and patterns.

Are You a Pomeranian Person?

S tately home or castle owner, apartment dweller, country bumpkin or city slicker, if you love happy little dogs with big personalities, you may well be just the person who would be a good Pomeranian owner. The author and her husband, truly quintessential Pom people, have owned Poms for over 40 years. We never tire of the breed's antics and cannot envision ourselves without a flock of Poms in the house.

Those who own Poms will attest that the breed is irresistible and many have trouble stopping at just one!

You just cannot become bored if there's a Pom in the house.

Because the Pomeranian is so small, you need not be a marathon runner to keep your dog fit, as so much exercise can be done in and around the home with very little effort on your part. Nonetheless, a Pom will always enjoy walks outdoors to discover new smells and to stimulate his super-active brain. This is where your sensible ownership comes into play. Always remember that your Pom is very tiny, so accidents can happen if you are not alert to the many dangers of the big wide world. Many Pom owners like to carry their bundles of canine fun around in special carriers. This is a great idea provided that you, as a careful owner, do not allow your Pom to jump out unexpectedly.

Poms are adaptable little fellows, but they do require certain accommodations. They will happily live in any

Pomeranian puppies are true little charmers in "ball-of-fluff" disguises.

The attention-loving Pom and the owner who wants to pamper him make a perfect pair.

CHAPTER 3

environment, but they don't fare very well in hot climates. Air conditioning is an essential if you live in a hot, humid environment. Another requirement is a fenced yard. Be sure the fence is Pom-proof. A 4-lb adult can slip through a chain-link fence with little effort; a puppy can walk through it! When in the yard, never tie your Pom out on a stake. He will have laryngitis before you bring him in, and your neighbors will soon become most un-neighborly. Be considerate and don't contribute to noise pollution.

Believe it or not, there are a couple of drawbacks to owning a Pomeranian. The author, after 40 years with the breed, can only come up with two. The first is that the Pom can be a noisy little guy. Poms are talkative folk; they have many ideas of their own and a keen desire to share their opinions. When you have a dozen or so of these in the house, as the author and her husband do, it can be rather annoying. Do not praise your Pom for barking; rather, correct him instantly. Once he quiets down, give him a toy or a treat (to occupy his mouth and brain).

The second drawback has to do with the Houdini element. As a member of the spitz family, the Pom is a professional escape artist and will not think twice about leaving the confines of your yard. This is an on-lead breed—don't even think about taking his leash off. Pom owners can't even spell "free run"!

Speaking of running, make no mistake—you better be pretty smart and on your toes to keep up with your little friend's intelligence. He is both dainty and quick, so you will need to be both quick-thinking and fairly nimble on your feet or he will run circles around you! If you, too, are dainty on your feet and dress in a rather flamboyant fashion, perhaps a ballet mistress at a stage school, for example, then you and your Pom will make a wonderfully complementary couple. Even so, the Pom appreciates sensible folk just as much as fancy extravagant ones. Joggers, ballplayers and other athletic types make great matches, too, as the Pom loves to be on the go.

Although abundant and potentially magnificent, the Pom's full double coat is not especially difficult to maintain in good condition. One of the biggest misunderstandings about the breed is that the coat is difficult to care for. You do not have to brush the Pom every day. In fact, correct coat texture is such that the coat should not be brushed too often. The author brushes her Poms about once a week or so. Your weekly brushing session should be pleasurable for you

and your Pom, for you will love spending time in each other's company. Your Pom will love you to bits if you spoil him, for Poms are just made to be spoiled. (Not too

As all colors are allowed in the Pom, coat-color choice is purely personal. Pom owners have quite a range to choose from.

much, though, as you'll live to regret that every day.) He will simply adore the attention, and you will, I hope, enjoy giving it.

As a perfect Pom owner, you will join in your little one's games and you will enjoy time spent sharing with and caring for your bundle of fluffy fun. Don't be fooled— under all that puff and fluff is a real dog who loves to have a good time.

Always keep in mind that

your Pomeranian is a member of the spitz family and, as such, he will be loyal to you and may be rather protective. If you are planning to have a party or strange visitors to your home, you might feel it wise to send out a complimentary pair of earmuffs with

Poms are show-offs, and events like flyball give them perfect opportunities to flaunt their agility and basic superiority.

each invitation, for your Pom is likely to bark at all of your guests.

Perhaps your interest lies in obedience training. In this case, you may well have found yourself a willing

canine partner who is a good learner and may allow you to show off a bit when he performs the odd trick or two that you have taught him. There's nothing kosher about the Pom: this is a real ham of a dog! His very nature is cocky, self-assured, confident and aware of his "specialness." If you don't like being the center of attention, you should think twice about owning this hammy spitz.

At dog shows, the ringside is enchanted by the Pom; in the park, at the shopping center, on Main Street, the Pom always draws a crowd. The very countenance of the Pom shouts out, "Hey, look me over! Look at ME!" That is what a Pom should be. He should never be spooky, snippy, meek or shy. The correct temperament of the breed is that of stage-center star, looking for the spotlight, smiling at the camera and enjoying the sighs of an admiring, applauding public.

For certain, your Pom will become your child, and you will soon refer to your dog as such. That said, owners with young children must be forewarned. If you have children in your home, or as regular visitors, you may want to think twice about owning a Pom, certainly while the children are small. This has nothing to do with the Pom's dislike for little people; in fact, Poms prefer fellow Lilliputians, but these are small dogs, *very* small dogs. Not until a Pom is eight or nine months of age can the dog be safe around toddlers. As a caring owner, you must

"Belly rub, please!" Pomeranians are not shy about asking for attention.

CHAPTER 3

The Pomeranian person wants a beautiful dog that is easy to maintain, of a small size yet sturdy and who is just brimming with person-ality that belies his compact stature.

keep this in mind. The responsibility of caring for a tiny breed is a huge one.

Children, even fairly well-behaved ones, might just treat a Pomeranian as they would a toy, and this can have disas-trous consequences. Likewise, Pom puppies are fast and can be wiggly, and will leap from a child's arms in an instant, possibly injuring themselves. Of course, if you are the proud mother or father of very gentle children and you have brought them up to respect everything they touch, then you may find that Poms fit in with your lifestyle, providing that the children and dogs are always under your close supervision.

If you are an owner of other animals, you will also have to consider very carefully whether or not a Pom will be suitable to join your family. How you introduce your pets will be an important part of that decision, but the personalities involved will have to be taken into consideration. You'll be glad to know that when a Pom does decide he's found a new doggie friend, or even a feline one, he will almost certainly build up a long-lasting and devoted relationship. Poms are not scrappy, in general, and get along well with other dogs. Perhaps a little clannish, they prefer the company of other Poms. A minor squabble between two males, or "words" over a favorite toy, is

26

an occasional occurrence, but for the most part Poms prefer a relaxed, laid-back home routine for themselves and their furry and human kin.

As we've said, the Pom is not a spooky type and is fairly fearless, unlike some of his fellow toys, who quake in the coolness of their own shadow. Poms will not recoil at the approach of a stranger and they will not back away from an encounter. Although the Pom is not a guard dog *per se*, it is an excellent watchdog and alarm dog. The author's home, protected by the eyes, ears and barks of a dozen Poms, is surely well protected.

When selecting any breed of dog, there is much to consider. If you think very carefully before making the decision to buy a Pomeranian, having weighed all the pros and cons, you can look forward to many years of happiness together—as well as lots of fun and games.

ARE YOU A POMERANIAN PERSON?

Overview

- The Pomeranian's compact size and adaptability make him ideal for almost any living environment, while his vibrant personality makes him appealing to many types of dog owners.
- Two "cons" of the breed are his tendencies to be vocal and to be an escape artist. You must keep your small dog's safety a top priority.
- The Pom's magnificent coat is not difficult for the pet owner to maintain in top condition.
- The Pom is active, smart and confident, able to achieve great successes in training and competition.
- Always supervise your tiny toy around children and other pets.

Selecting a Breeder

Whether you are selecting a Pomeranian as a home companion, walking mate, show dog or competition dog, you positively need to find a good breeder whose main breed (likely only breed) is the Pomeranian. Even if you're seeking "only a pet," you want a Pom that looks like a Pom, acts how a Pom acts and is as healthy and sound as any Best-in-Show winner. Because the breed ranks high in popularity,

Each litter and each tiny puppy represents a dedicated breeder's efforts, research, time, planning and love of the breed...you owe it to yourself and the breed to find such a breeder.

there are hundreds of breeders out there: some are fabulous, some are acceptable, some are not as good as the others. Given the small size of Pomeranian litters (sometimes only one or two puppies), it takes even more litters and breeders to register the same number of puppies as it would for a larger breed (which can have as many as 10 or 12 puppies in a single litter). You must be very particular and not simply settle for the litter bred closest to your home. You will live with this choice for the next 12 to 15 years.

At a dog show you can find experienced breeders and have the opportunity to meet their show dogs and future sires and dams.

Reputable breeders must comply with the code of ethics set down by their breed club. There are national and regional breed clubs in different countries, though all of them require adherence to their codes. The American Pomeranian Club stipulates that members' dogs may not be used at stud on unregistered bitches, while a club in Canada insists that its members sell all pets (i.e., not show dogs) on a

Your road to the perfect pup begins with doing your homework to find a reputable, ethical breeder.

Canadian Kennel Club non-breeding agreement and/or spay/neuter contract. So, when selecting the breeder, you are wise to choose one who is a club member in good standing.

Visit the American Pomeranian Club's website at www.americanpomeranian club.org. There you will find an excellent breeder referral service categorized by state. Only the member breeders who request to be on the list will be found there, but it is certainly a superb starting point for your breeder search. There's a Canadian section as well.

Prospective puppy buyers should always keep foremost in their minds that not all breeders have the breed's interests at heart; some are less dedicated. It is essential that you locate one that has not only dogs you admire but also breeding ethics with which you can agree. Select a breeder who breeds to the standard, who has a real reason for breeding the bitch and who has been "in Poms"

for at least a decade.

Caring breeders always want to know everything possible about their prospective puppy parents. You will be able to tell if your Pom breeder is such a person from the first meeting. He should be interested in you, your lifestyle, your home environment, your dog-owning experience, your family and maybe even your income. Don't be offended. The more detailed the interrogation, the more that breeder cares about his puppies. Such a breeder doesn't bargain with his puppies! He is not out to make a sale: he's out to find a home for one of his cherished kids.

There are many good breeders around and if you look carefully, you will find just such a person. If you can be personally recommended to someone, that is an ideal start, but you still need to be sure that the breeder's standards of care are what you would expect. You must also be as certain as you can be that the breeder fully understands the breed and has given careful consideration to the way the Pomeranian has been bred, taking into account the pedigrees and genetic health of each Pom he uses for breeding.

The breeder you select may be someone who breeds from home, in which case the puppies will have hopefully been brought up in the house and will be familiar with all the activities and noises of a human family. However, the breeder may run a large establishment, so that the litter has perhaps been raised in a kennel situation. Still, if you have chosen wisely, the puppies will have had lots of human contact and exposure to various sights and sounds. Even some of the larger breeding establishments whelp litters inside the home, and in my personal opinion this is infinitely better than having puppies raised entirely in a kennel environment, especially for small breeds such as the Pomeranian.

However large or small the breeding establishment, it is important that the conditions in which the puppies are raised are suitable. The areas should be clean and the puppies

A proud mom watches over her brood. Being small dogs, Poms produce small litters, so you must be patient in your breeder and puppy search.

should be well supervised in a suitable environment. All should look in tiptop condition and temperaments should be sound, the puppies full of fun and with plenty of confidence.

The breeder should be perfectly willing to show you the dam, and it will be interesting for you to take careful note of her own temperament and how she interacts with her offspring. Bear in mind that the dam may not look her "Best of Breed" best. She's been tending a demanding brood, so her coat may look less glamorous than you might expect. Nonetheless, she should still be in good health, approachable and proud in that unmistakable motherly way. If the dam is not available for you to see, be warned that this might be a sign that the litter was not born on the premises, but has been brought in to be sold, which would be your cue to keep searching.

As for the stud dog, it is likely that he will not be available, for he may well be owned by someone else, and a careful breeder may have traveled hundreds of miles to use his stud services. Most likely, the breeder will be able to show you a picture of him (hopefully winning at a show), or at least will show you his pedigree and tell you about him. If you've never looked at a pedigree before, you can eye it with the following in mind: the breeder's kennel name usually should be evident by looking at the pedigree. For example, the author's kennel name, Jeribeth, is used in all dogs that we have bred. A good pedigree is linebred, which means that you will see the kennel name in about half of the names on the pedigree. Look for a few "Ch." prefixes before the parents' and/or grandparents' names, possibly even the great-grandparents' names; if the only "Ch." is further back than the great-grandparents, it is essentially meaningless. You can look for "CD" suffixes, which indicate the obedience potential of the dogs, or other suffixes. Ask the breeder to explain the different suffixes. If you see no prefixes or suffixes, you probably are at a hobby breeder who doesn't show or compete with his dogs. This is far from ideal.

A well-chosen breeder will be able to give the new puppy

owner lots of useful guidance, including advice about feeding. Some breeders give a small quantity of food to the new owners when the puppy leaves home; in any event, they should always provide written details of exactly what type and quantity of food has been fed, and with what regularity. You will, of course, be able to change this as time goes on, but the change must be gradual.

A breeder will also need to tell you what vaccinations the puppy has received, and all health documentation should be handed over at the time of purchase. Details about the puppy's worming routine must also be made clear. Ask about any health guarantee as part of the sales contract. Many breeders also provide temporary insurance coverage for the puppy. This is an especially good idea, and the new owner can subsequently decide whether or not to continue with this particular policy.

SELECTING A BREEDER

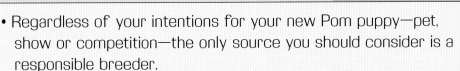

Overview

- Regardless of your intentions for your new Pom puppy—pet, show or competition—the only source you should consider is a responsible breeder.
- The American Pomeranian Club is a trusted source from which to obtain breeder referrals and information about Pom ownership.
- Your chosen breeder should follow high standards in his breeding ethics and the care of his dogs, including having all necessary health testing done on breeding stock before the breeding takes place.
- The breeder will have many questions for and requirements of you.
- A good breeder will review pedigrees with you and will provide you with all necessary documentation should he agree to sell you a puppy.

Finding the Right Puppy

Who can resist a puppy bundle of Pomeranian joy? If you love Poms, every puppy you meet on your search inevitably will melt your heart. Of course, a puppy reared in ideal conditions, clean quarters and a happy, stable environment will be far more appealing than a puppy that has not been looked after so well.

Find out whether or not the breeder has screened the litter's sire and dam for potential problems that are common in the breed; he should be happy to show you such documentation. The Pomeranian is usually a healthy little dog, but some problems do raise their heads from time to time, so it is wise to know

Curious and alert from puppyhood, the Pomeranian pup is a fun and fluffy friend.

that your pup comes from healthy stock. Luxating patella can be a problem, as can hypothyroidism, collapsing trachea and male-predominant alopecia. Some Pomeranians have also been found to have idiopathic epilepsy. This typically occurs between the ages of three and seven years, and it is thought to be inherited. Hypoglycemia is also a concern with toy dogs like the Pom. Ask the breeder about the occurrence of genetic eye and/or heart disease in his line.

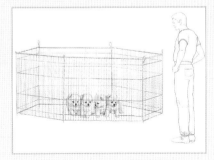

The breeder will show you the litter so that you can watch the pups in action, interacting with you and with their littermates, to get to know their individual differences.

The American Pomeranian Club supports a Canine Health Foundation grant to find a DNA marker for alopecia in the breed. The hereditary condition known as male-predominant alopecia results in hair loss in affected animals. It is also called "black skin" disease. Ask your breeder about the incidence of this disease in his line. Breeders will not breed any dog that is affected by this type of alopecia. Currently there is disagreement among Pom breeders about the cause, cure and hereditary aspect of the disease.

The outgoing and happy nature of the breed should shine in the expression of every Pom.

A healthy puppy should strike you as being clean, without any sign of discharge from the eyes or nose. His rear end should be spotless, with no indication of loose stool. Although any puppy's nails can be sharp, they should not be overly long; tidy nails indicate that the breeder has clipped them as necessary.

The pup's coat should be in excellent condition and there should be absolutely no sign of parasites. Parasites such as fleas and lice cannot always be seen easily, but will be indicated by the puppy's scratching. You also might notice a rash. Fleas can do great damage to a puppy's skin and coat, so cleanliness is an important consideration.

Scratching, though, does not always indicate a parasitic or skin condition, for it can also be associated with teething. In this case, the puppy will only scratch around his head area. When the second set of teeth have come through so that the gums are no longer sore, this type of scratching will stop. Scratching might also be connected with an ear infection, so take a quick look inside your new puppy's ears. Of course, a good breeder will have a vet certify that the puppy is in good health before offering him for sale.

Most healthy puppies are outgoing and fun-loving, so do not take pity on the overly shy one that hides away in a corner. When you go to select your puppy, you should take with you the members of your family with whom the puppy will spend time at home. It is essential that every one in the family agrees with the important decision you are about to make, for a new puppy will inevitably change your lives.

Hopefully you will have done plenty of research about the breed long before reaching the stage of having a new puppy enter your lives. When surfing the Internet, be aware that not every website is as valid and accurate as the next. It's best to rely on the websites of breed clubs and/or breeders whose reputation you trust. Breed clubs are also important sources of help and information. Some even publish their own leaflets and booklets about the breed and might even publish a book of champions so that you can look back to see what your puppy's famous ancestors actually looked like. You may also consider subscribing to a canine periodical, such as the *Pomeranian Review*, published by the American Pomeranian Club, the *Pom Reader* or *Dog World* or *Dogs in Review*.

Finally, it is a good idea to become a member of at least one breed club. In doing so, you will stay abreast of Pomeranian events and meet others who share your love of the breed, thus providing ongoing opportunities to learn about the Pomeranian. If you've never been to a dog show, you should make an effort to attend one. It's an educational and enjoyable experience, and you might even decide to enter your Pomeranian in a match.

FINDING THE RIGHT PUPPY

Overview

- Every Pom pup you meet will steal your heart, but you must use your head in making your puppy selection.
- When you visit the litter, all pups should look healthy and be friendly.
- Aside from just appearing healthy, the pups must actually *be* healthy. The breeder should show you documentation of all health and genetic testing done on the parents and, where applicable, on the pups.
- Have fun meeting the litter and observing the pups' personalities. Make your visit a family affair so that everyone has a part in the decision.

Welcoming the Pomeranian

After you have found the right breeder and selected your puppy, you likely will have several days or even weeks to wait until your Pom is old enough to join you in your home. Most breeders do not release Pom puppies until they are 12 weeks of age, sometimes older, although you will be able to visit the litter and make your selection before then. Every day you have to wait will seem like an eternity, but

Despite his bold outlook on life, the Pom is still a tiny creature in a big world. Help him adjust when he first comes home; this should not take much time.

make good use of the time. You will have lots of preparations to make. For the momentous day when your Pomeranian arrives home, you will want to be certain that everything at home is as well prepared as it can possibly be.

When visiting with the breeder, you should have ample opportunity to discuss exactly what your puppy will need to make his life healthy, safe and also enjoyable. Depending on where you live, you will probably have easy access to one of the large pet-supply stores or a good privately owned shop. Both types of store should be staffed by knowledgeable individuals who know about dogs and can recommend which products are best suited for toy dogs. Sometimes smaller supply shops are owned by people who show their own dogs, in which case they often have a wide range of items and will probably be able to give sensible guidance as to what you need to buy.

With his confident and outgoing nature, the Pom puppy should feel right at home before you know it.

The crate that you purchase for your puppy should be of adequate size to house him as an adult.

You must plan where the puppy is to sleep, but there are many other things to think about, too. Hopefully the breeder will already have given you guidance as to the feeding regimen, so you should purchase a bag of the food you plan to feed. The puppy's food will change as he matures, so don't buy out the pet-supply store! Select the "small-bite" kibble, made especially for tiny mouths. The breeder may or may not have advised you to mix the kibble with a canned food.

Another critical item to find is the Pom's crate. Purchase a small wire crate and a nice soft (machine-washable) crate pad. Both of these items will be easy to find at a pet-supply store.

You will need some grooming equipment for your Pomeranian. At this early stage, you will need to purchase a high-quality wide-toothed comb and a natural bristle brush as well as a pair of grooming scissors and a guillotine-type nail clipper. You also should purchase a good-quality doggie shampoo and condi- tioner. Do not purchase a wire slicker brush or a nylon brush, as these will break the Pom's hair. Take the breeder's advice as to which particular kinds of grooming tools he recommends. If taking your Pom to a professional groomer, discuss from the outset which grooming tools he will be using and inform him of your breeder's sugges- tions. You will need additional items like cotton swabs, cotton balls, towels and a styptic stick (for stanching minor cuts), which you probably already have on hand as household items.

The wire crate is popular for use indoors because it provides a safe den for your Pom while giving him a clear view of what's going on around him.

Other puppy necessities include a lightweight yet sturdy leash and collar, bowls for food and water, ID tags and a few safe toys. Again, you should have all of the basics on hand before puppy comes home.

Now let's talk about your Pom's sleeping arrangements. On the first night, you will be so excited about your new charge that you will want to carry him to bed with you. This may sound like a harmless idea, but it's not. Where your Pom puppy sleeps on the first night (and every night afterward) is a major consideration. It is only natural that the newcomer will be restless for the first couple of nights or so, but it is time to introduce him to his crate. Many good breeders expose puppies to crates before they leave for their new homes; if you have found such a breeder, *wunderbar*! If not, then now is the appointed time to

begin crate-training your new charge.

Place the puppy in his wire crate with the soft padding, close the door and say "Good night, Gracie." If you feel compelled, or if the

puppy is whining dramatically, place the crate in your bedroom next to your bed. He will hear and smell you, he will know that you're nearby, and that is enough to quiet him down. Let's repeat this one more time: do not pick that 1-pound bundle up, cuddle him and put him in your bed. You will regret this for the next 15 years—yes,

The Pom is gregarious and enjoys the company of other dogs, especially other Poms, but all introductions should be made carefully and the dogs supervised with each other as their friendship develops.

A Pom in a
basket makes
a lovely
picture, but a
wicker
basket is not
a suitable as
a bed or as a
carrier.

Most Poms enjoy crunchy dog biscuits, but remember that they have tiny mouths and teeth, so choose treats that they can handle.

that's longer than some marriages today! Yee-ha!

Once the puppy is reliably house-trained, you can purchase a nice dog bed. Placing the bed in a central location in your home, like the family room or den, is ideal. Visit a pet-supply shop or look at an online catalog to see the wide array of doggie beds available. Select one that you think captures the personality of your Pom—and then take lots of photos of your pampered pooch lounging in luxury!

A word of warning: wicker beds may look pretty, but they are dangerous because puppies chew them and sharp wicker pieces can all too easily injure eyes, get entangled in the coat or be swallowed. It is wiser to choose a durable bed that can be washed or wiped down. A hard-sided bed can easily be lined with comfortable soft bedding that can be washed frequently, for it will be important that all of your dog's bedding is kept clean and dry. You should also choose a bed that is either just slightly raised from the ground or else positioned so that it will avoid drafts.

Although a Pomeranian is very small, this is an active breed that can get into all kinds of mischief. Everyday household items may seem harmless enough, but a dainty cloth draped over the side of a little table full of fragile ornaments is just asking for trouble. Even more dangerous to a mischievous puppy are electric wires, so be sure they are concealed from his reach. Tiny teeth can bite through all too easily, causing a potentially fatal accident. Another word of warning concerns household chemicals including cleaning agents and gardening aids. Many of these items contain substances that are poisonous, so please keep them out of the way of a curious Pom. The same goes for sharp tools that could cause injury.

When your puppy first arrives home, it is only natural that you will be excited to show your new-found companion to your friends. Don't make too much of a fuss too soon. Your puppy is making a big move in his short life, so the first two or three days are best spent quietly at home with you and your family. When

Children and Poms are not always a perfect match. As accidents can happen in play, albeit inadvertently, supervision between children and your dog is always recom-mended.

44

your puppy has found his feet and taken stock of his new surroundings, you will be able to introduce him to lots of new people and experiences. If you have young children, or if they visit, always carefully supervise any time spent with your young puppy. Youngsters are often attracted by the colorful coat of a Pomeranian, and little fingers can all too easily tug at the coat and hurt the puppy, even with the best of intentions.

If your family has other pets, or if your pup will be meeting other people's pets, introductions should be made slowly and under close supervision. Most Pomeranians get along well with other animals, but you should always exercise caution until you are certain that all concerned are going to be the best of friends.

WELCOMING THE POMERANIAN

Overview

- Use your time wisely while awaiting your Pom pup's arrival home. There are many supplies to buy and things to do around the house to make it a safe, puppy-proof place.
- Among the items you will need are puppy food and bowls, a crate, grooming equipment, a collar and leash, ID tags and toys.
- Choose your pup's sleeping arrangements carefully, as the habits you instill now will last a lifetime.
- All kinds of puppy dangers lurk in the home, among them electrical cords, household chemicals and breakable items.
- Your pup's first few days should be low-key, with puppy getting to know the family and becoming accustomed to his new surroundings.

House-training Your Pomeranian

Although there are very occasional exceptions, most dogs like to be clean in their toileting habits. Until house-training is complete, however, accidents will inevitably happen, so be prepared. As you get to know your Pom puppy better, you will recognize when he needs to go out because you will have learned his signs. Initially, though, the signals he gives may not be very clear, or you might just not be around when he casts a quick

Once learned, the toileting routine will be just another part of your Pom's day.

glance at the door handle. To house-train with success, you will need to be consistent and ready at all times.

Discipline in house-training has no place. When your dog makes a mess, you may be aggravated (even angry), but your puppy will not be able to compute this emotion correctly. (He doesn't much care for puddles either.) He in time will comprehend that he has disappointed you (somehow), but in order to correct house-training mistakes, you must catch him *in the act*. That is to say, actually in mid-piddle or mid-poo. Even then, there's not much the puppy can do except finish what he (unfortunately) already started.

When your puppy first arrives home, he may or may not have been started on a house-training routine, albeit to a limited extent, if the breeder introduced the puppy to a crate. Crate-training is discussed in more detail in Chapter 11 and is

With a small dog, some owners, especially those who live in cities, like to start out with paper-training, eventually progressing to outdoor toilet training.

It doesn't take a large crate to fit a pair of Poms, but, for house-training purposes and indoor use, each dog needs his own individual crate, his own private "home within a home."

the most reliable way to achieve house-training success. Regardless of your pup's crate experience, you must always realize that your home is completely different from the breeder's, so he will have to relearn the house rules and learn a new schedule. Doors will not

A Pom who is accustomed to using his crate will accept confinement for safety wherever you go. An ex-pen serves as a useful tool during travel.

be located in the same places, the floor plan is different, your family may go to bed and rise at different times, and it will undoubtedly take him a little

time to learn and to adapt.

The speed of your house-training success will depend to a certain extent on your living environment and on the season of the year. Most puppies are perfectly happy to go out into the yard in nice dry weather, but when rain is pouring down on a cold winter morning, many feel rather differently and will need considerable encouragement. Likewise, snow complicates house-training considerably. If your puppy can't traverse the snowy banks to find his potty spot, there's not much you can do to help (other than shovel a path or at least a good clearing).

Paper-training can be useful in the very early stages of training, especially in the winter months or if you live in a high-rise apartment or if you don't have a fenced back yard. The paper should be placed by the door so that the dog learns to associate the paper with the exit to the wide world outside. Whenever he uses the paper, he should be praised. Obviously, it is ideal if the puppy can be taken outside as soon as he shows any sign of wanting "to go," but you may not always be able to grab the leash and get him out the door in time.

Remember that puppies need to go out much more frequently than adult animals, certainly immediately after being released from their crates, after naps and following meals. In fact, taking a young puppy outside every hour while he is awake is not a bad idea at all. Always keep both your eyes and ears open, and your shoes on, for a youngster will not be able to wait those extra two minutes until you are ready to take him out. Also look into puppy pads (available at pet shops) that can really simplify your housebreaking

plan. As your puppy matures, his "asking" to be let out when necessary will become second nature, and it is rare to encounter a Pomeranian that is deliberately unclean in the house. A stud dog, however, can be

A clean Pom is a happy Pom! Do your part in keeping him clean by always picking up after him, whether in your yard or out in public.

different, for he may well want to mark his territory, and your table and chair legs may be just the places he chooses. Marking is different from urinating and cannot be cured by house-training methods.

Simple one-word commands are very helpful: "Outside" and "Potty" are favorites, and either seems to work just fine. Never, ever forget to give praise when the deed is done in the desired place. However, if an accident happens, you indeed should give a verbal reprimand, but remember that this will only work if your Pomeranian is caught *in the act*. If you try to reprimand him after the event, even just five seconds after, he will simply not know what he has done wrong and will only become confused.

It is essential that any mess is cleaned up immediately. If your dog has done his business in the wrong place, you must clean it up thoroughly with a product made to eliminate the odor or else your puppy will want to use that particular place again. When your puppy is old enough to be exercised in public places, always carry with you a "pooper-

House-trained dogs can be given more freedom in the house, as you don't have to worry constantly about potty accidents occurring.

scoop" or small plastic bags so that any mess can be picked up. Many towns have local ordinances requiring owners to clean up after their pets, so abide by these laws and be a responsible dog owner. The anti-dog lobby exists in every community, so please give them no cause for complaint.

Popping up to say hi! Yet another benefit of crate-training is that your Poms will be comfortable when traveling. They will certainly enjoy accompanying you whenever possible.

HOUSE-TRAINING YOUR POMERANIAN

Overview

- Poms are smart little dogs who like to be clean in their habits and thus should housebreak fairly easily if you are consistent.
- Crate-training is the most reliable way to house-train a dog, although some owners of small dogs start out with paper-training.
- Get on a schedule of taking your pup out frequently for relief. He will learn to tell you when he needs to go out, and you will learn to recognize his signs.
- Praise your Pom when he "goes" in the desired area. Never scold him for having an accident indoors unless you actually catch him in the act.
- You are teaching your dog to be clean, and you must be clean, too! Clean up all accidents indoors thoroughly and always pick up any droppings outdoors.

Feeding Your Pomeranian

Until your Pomeranian is six months of age, you should feed him at least three or four times per day. Because the Pomeranian puppy has such a tiny mouth, it is very important that the dry food you select is of the "small-bite" variety. Many Pomeranian owners keep their Poms on puppy food even into adulthood. This is usually higher in protein than a food designed for adults, but because this is an active little breed, many breeders feel that this suits a Pom well throughout the dog's life. When serving the dry food,

Along with a good-quality food, a constant supply of water is essential to the Pom's health. Water should always be available for your Pom.

moisten it with a little warm water or low-salt chicken broth. Any of the premium brands sold in pet shops are suitable for Poms. In addition to the dry kibble, you should offer your Pom a little raw ground beef, the leaner the better. The author prefers ground chuck or ground round. Add a little cottage cheese to the pup's portions as well. This helps to firm up the Pom's stools. For variety, you can add some human baby food, like strained lamb, beef or chicken. There's no such thing as a too-fat baby Pom, though there are lots of fat adult Poms out there.

A bowl full of food and a jar full of treats make for a happy Pomeranian.

PREMIUM FOODS

Always feed according to the manu-facturer's instructions. If you have a reluctant eater, you may have to add the cottage cheese, baby food or raw ground meat to each meal instead of just one or two. The premium dry foods are truly balanced, thanks to

The young littermates are started on solid food by the breeder as part of the weaning process. This is a true "family style" puppy dinner.

modern canine science, so additional supplementation is not necessary. Only supplement under the advisement and guidance of your vet.

Today there is an enormous range of specially prepared foods available for dogs, many of them scientifically balanced and suitable for various age ranges and breed sizes. Selecting a brand of premium food can be overwhelming, since there are many major companies that produce dozens of varieties.

Because of the range of products available, you may find it difficult to decide which to choose without advice from another Pomeranian enthusiast. Experiment to find the brand your Pom likes. It is really a matter of personal (and Pomeranian) preference as to which particular food you decide to use, though initially you will be influenced by the brand and variety of food that has been fed to your new puppy by his breeder. Changes can, of course, be made to this, but never change suddenly from one food to another or your Pomeranian is likely to get an upset tummy. Introduce a new brand of food gradually over a few days, increasing the ratio of new food to old until the old brand is phased out. There is usually no harm at all in changing the flavor of food while keeping with the same brand.

Dry food should be stored carefully, bearing in mind that its vitamin value declines if not used fairly quickly, usually within about three months. It is also essential that a plentiful supply of fresh water is available for your Pom at all times.

TREAT TIPS
Be mindful of not giving your Pom table scraps for a host

of good reasons. First, many human foods cannot be digested by dogs, and some can be toxic. For example, chocolate, especially dark chocolate, is carcinogenic to dogs, as are onions, the pits and seeds of certain fruits and anything with caffeine or alcohol. Grapes, raisins and nuts are also big no-nos. Second, feeding a dog from the table teaches him to beg, which is a nuisance of a problem that is difficult to correct. Finally, human foods can put weight on a Pom, which is imperceptible at first (well hidden by a blooming coat). Even 1 extra pound on a 3-pound dog is a huge problem, and Jenny Craig doesn't answer the phone when your Pom calls.

A low-cal treat between meals, however, is another story! Our adult Poms love milk biscuits, but they are too hard for puppies. Adults also will enjoy a knuckle bone. A fairly large bone is best, and never offer chicken, pork or fish bones.

ADULT MEALS

How many times a day you feed your adult Pomeranian will probably be a matter of

Use treats wisely, remembering that the extra calories add up quickly, especially with such a small dog.

preference. Unlike larger dogs, Poms need to eat often, as hunger can cause serious problems in a Pomeranian. Most owners feed a morning and evening meal, plus a little light lunch and a couple of "snacks" or treats. Obviously, puppies need to be fed more frequently, and the transition to the adult meal plan should be made gradually.

Once the Pom is one year of age, you should present his meal to him and leave it down for 20 or 25 minutes. If he hasn't eaten it or finished it after that time, pick it up and discard it. Do not leave

Sturdy plastic or stainless steel bowls are fine for your Pom's food and water. Get small-sized, shallow bowls for your tiny dog.

the food sitting around all day, available for whenever your little finicky fellow decides to nibble. If your Pom finishes his food off right away, you can add a little more, but if he eats his fill and there's some left over, you're probably feeding too much. In no time, your Pom will become a better, more

consistent eater, which is what you want.

Keep in mind that you don't want a porky Pom. An overweight grown-up is not healthy; obesity can even take years off a dog's life. Under that abundant adult coat, you still should be able to see your Pom's waist. Don't overfeed. Poms are not greedy eaters, so obesity in Poms has more to do with fatty treats than their eating too much at mealtimes.

HYPOGLYCEMIA ALERT
That your Pom eats well regularly is critical to his health. Poms are subject to hypoglycemia, brought on by the blood sugar's sinking too low. Some breeders call these stress attacks or weak spells, but they are caused by the Pom's not eating enough or

not drinking enough water. Remember, that water bowl must be available at all times (even through the house-training process). If you do not recognize the signs of your Pom suffering from a hypoglycemia attack, he could die. Signs of the attack include the puppy's lying on his side, eyes rolled back or closed, in a semi-catatonic state. Your response must be immediate: you transform into the Candyman! Your Pom needs to swallow water with a little sugar, honey or corn syrup.

The author's secret, which she happily shares, is Nutrical®, which comes in a tube and is filled with calories, nutrients and vitamins. Poms think of it as candy. It's a brown gel that the puppy can lick directly from the tube; usually about an inch is enough. For young puppies, we give them a lick once or twice a day. If your Pom puppy is looking a little droopy, it's time for an extra little Nutrical® boost!

FEEDING YOUR POMERANIAN

Overview

- A puppy diet should consist of a small-bite puppy food; a few extras, like a bit of raw beef and cottage cheese, are good for the young Pom.
- When choosing the Pom's diet, prepare to be overwhelmed! Take advice from your breeder and vet, and choose a food designed for toy breeds.
- Some "people foods" are toxic to dogs and others can cause stomach upset, so it's best to avoid feeding table scraps as a rule. You also want to keep your dog at a healthy weight and not encourage him to beg.
- Watch your dog's condition and appetite to determine portions to feed.
- Be aware that Poms can become hypoglycemic and know how to deal with it at the first symptoms.

CHAPTER 9

Keeping Your Pomeranian Active

The Pomeranian is such a tiny breed that you will inevitably have to pay special attention to where you exercise your little canine friend. However, regular exercise is very important to keep your pet in good health, both bodily and mentally. You may decide to take him out for regular walks, but if you have a sizable fenced yard, regular play sessions in this enclosed area may be suitable as an alternative. Having said that, a Pomeranian will always appreciate a walk with his owner. This is a time for

The playful Pom will enjoy time in the house with his favorite toys.

investigating new places and new smells, keeping his senses alert.

When walking your Pom, it is best to keep him on lead. Some Pomeranians, when really well trained, are fairly obedient off lead, but this is truly the exception and not worth the risk. Owners must keep foremost in mind that this is a small dog, so accidents might just happen when they encounter larger, heavier dogs whom they do not know. Poms are fearless and will not back down from an encounter. Fearlessness is one thing—getting picked up by a surly German Shepherd is quite another! Keep an eye on your Pom whenever he's meeting (or trying to intimidate) a canine giant.

Upon returning indoors from any outdoor time with your Pom, it is essential to remove all debris from his coat. It is also important not to leave the coat wet following exercise on damp ground.

Poms make wonderful therapy dogs, visiting nursing homes and cheering up the elderly and infirm patients.

Up and over the dog walk! The little Pom's intelligence and energy make him a natural at agility training and competition.

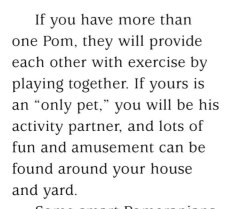

Flying high! Well, not that high... In obedience and agility, jumps are adjusted to the size of the dog.

If you have more than one Pom, they will provide each other with exercise by playing together. If yours is an "only pet," you will be his activity partner, and lots of fun and amusement can be found around your house and yard.

Some smart Pomeranians are now used in therapy work, visiting homes and hospitals to meet the residents and patients, bringing cuddles and companionship. The breed's convenient size and lively person-ality make these

visits something to which the elderly and the infirm greatly look forward. Therapy work is a superb occasion for the Pom to take center stage! It is also not unknown for a Pomeranian to become a "hearing dog," a live-in assistance dog for the hearing impaired. This is a dog that is specially trained to listen for sounds like telephones and doorbells ringing, something of great assistance to a deaf owner.

Because the Pom is one smart little dog, it's not uncommon to see the breed participating in obedience trials. Poms have had a presence in the sport since the 1940s. The first Pom to earn the Utility Dog degree did so in an obedience trial in 1943; this was Georgian's Betty, owned by Mrs. Agnes Niven.

Agility trials have become popular with Poms since the 1990s. These obstacle-course events are a perfect match for the versatile, quick-thinking and active Pomeranian and his like-minded owner. Many Poms have earned titles in these types of performance event. Ollie Blue Bluster, bred by Ray Mooney and owned by R. and R. Griffith Morris, earned three performance titles, in obedience, tracking and agility. Ollie is a great example of how limitless the Pom's abilities can be!

Even if your Pom does not take part in any of these activities, you can enjoy endless hours of fun together. When not sleeping or relaxing, he will enjoy playing games with you and his safe toys. Rubber balls and rawhide are other Pom favorites. Always remember, though, that toys should be checked regularly to ensure that no loose parts might be swallowed or cause injury. It is easy for pieces of rawhide to be swallowed so rawhides should be offered under supervision only.

KEEPING YOUR POMERANIAN ACTIVE

Overview

- Walks with you and free play in a fenced enclosure are good ways to keep the Pom's body moving and mind stimulated.
- Think safety first with your tiny toy when exercising him in public places.
- Poms make good therapy dogs, as they are small, are friendly and love the attention. They also can make good assistance dogs.
- Poms enjoy obedience and agility and are very capable of achieving success in both types of competition.
- Your Pomeranian's favorite way to stay active is by doing things with his favorite people.

Grooming Your Pomeranian

Don't let the Pom's glorious full coat fool you. This is an easy-care dog that doesn't need long daily grooming sessions. While the author brushes her Poms about once a week or so, some owners will brush their dogs every other day. Daily brushing is too much. The adult's coat truly can look like a picture, but the coat does not maintain itself entirely. Of course, if you have purchased a well-bred Pom, the adult's proper harsh coat texture makes it easier to keep up.

Your tiny Pom puppy will just look like a ball of fluff at first, but

The Pom's dark eyes glistening, surrounded by a lovely mane of hair, creates a look that has attracted so many to the breed.

remember that his coat will change considerably as he grows into adulthood. The adult's coat should be harsh, straight and glistening. Although a Pom's coat is not especially difficult to look after, regular grooming sessions will be an important aspect of canine care and you should check over the coat on a daily basis, with longer grooming sessions scheduled two or three times each week.

The tail is one of the Pom's hallmark features. It is brushed over the back, toward the head, to accentuate the full plume.

COAT CARE

Your Pomeranian's double coat consists of a soft dense undercoat and a long straight outer coat that stands off from the dog's body due to the thickness of the undercoat. The magnificence of this coat is not only in its sheer abundance—a Pom in full coat looks like a wonderful puffball—but also in the frill extending from the neck over the shoulders and chest. For all its splendor, the coat

For the puppy, gentle strokes with a bristle brush are all that is required. Your main goal is to accustom him to the process of being groomed.

sheds moderately; it is the undercoat that blows out in a white fuzz all over your clothes and furniture. During the twice-annual shedding times, usually in spring and autumn, you will find small colonies of "Pom fuzz bunnies" whirling around your floors. At these times, daily grooming is called for and can help control the amount of hair wafting around your home. Do not neglect to groom the coat during these shedding periods or the dead coat can form tangles and mats that are difficult to remove.

It is essential that short grooming sessions begin at an early age. Even within the first three or four days of owning your new puppy, a few minutes daily should be set aside, teaching the little one to stand on a solid table and accept grooming very gently. Use a good natural bristle brush (never a wire or nylon brush, as these can damage the coat). Brush all the way down to the skin. At first your puppy may object to this, but soon he will get used to being brushed and begin to enjoy it. Always talk to the youngster to put him at his ease and soon he will grow to look forward to the experience.

When the puppy reaches his adolescent stage (usually around four to six months of age), he will begin to lose his soft puppy coat and start to look quite naked. For a while, your beautiful puppy will resemble a homely street urchin. (Some breeders call this stage the "uglies.") Have faith! Beauty is just around the corner. He will be even more lovely when his adult coat emerges.

Grooming sessions will lengthen in time with maturity of the coat. Your Pom will have grown his full adult coat by about 18 months of age, from which time the coats of males remain pretty much the same throughout their lives, apart from shedding times. Unspayed bitches, however, will almost invariably lose coat from time to time due to hormonal changes, and following a litter it can take several months for a bitch's

removal of too much coat and will prevent hair breakage.

Brush the coat out in sections, using your natural bristle brush. Some people

The result of trimming the Pom's coat should be a rounded appearance, resembling a ball.

coat to get back into top condition.

Never groom a Pom's coat when it is absolutely dry. Use a fine water spray or coat dressing, or even a mixture of water and conditioner; any of these will help avoid the

prefer a pin brush, but the author prefers the bristle brush. To impart that all-important finishing touch, you can comb through carefully with a good-quality wide-toothed comb.

You must always be certain

that your grooming equipment is kept clean so that it does not cause the hair to snag. Take care, too, that you do not mistakenly use a comb with missing teeth, for this can damage the coat and can even catch the skin.

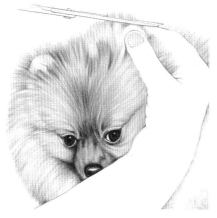

Trimming the ears can be tricky. Instead of following the shape of the ear, a straight cut across is recommended, being careful not to cut the leather.

A Pom's coat should always be groomed in an upward direction, from tail to neck, and the neck ruff itself should be brushed outwards. Be sure that breeching at the back is brushed away from the anus, and remember to groom the tail plume very carefully indeed. Keep the Pom's eyes and mouth clean with a damp cotton wipe or wash cloth.

TRIMMING

An over-trimmed Pomeranian can look completely alien, so do watch more experienced owners carefully and learn as much as you can about their methods. On the other hand, an undertrimmed Pom can also look most unattractive. You will need to strike that happy medium.

Keep in mind that a Pom should look like a ball. The chest must be rounded; so too must be breechings at the back. The breechings should blend with the tail plume over the back. Pomeranian trimming should be a simple procedure. Expert show trimming comes with experience, but novices can approach the trimming by following a few basic recommendations.

Trim all excess hair from across the tops of the ears, being careful not to cut into the ear leather. A nice straight line cut across the top looks better than trying to follow the contour of the ear. You don't want a "pointed" look. Clip all excess hair from between the toes and from under the bottom of the feet and foot pads. Then scissor a nice round "cat's paw," leaving no long hair. The area under the tail, around the rectal opening, should be kept trimmed for sanitary reasons. With practice, you can clip a circular area around the size of a quarter, or a bit larger for an adult.

Part of grooming should always include your Pom's bottom. You must check your Pom's rectal area every day for dried fecal matter that can cling to the hair and skin. If undetected, this can cause serious trouble. Often a young puppy can become soiled on his bottom to the extent that it's impossible for him to eliminate. In order to clean your Pom's bottom, simply hold his rear quarters under warm running water and wash the area with soap and water. Blot it dry with paper towels.

Remember to check it every day. He'll be more comfortable and smell better, too.

BATHING

Show Poms are usually bathed before each exhibition. When their dogs are not being shown, some owners like to bathe them every other week,

Have a heavy towel close by during your Pom's bath so you can wrap him in the towel and lift him out of the tub or basin.

some even less frequently. Before putting your Pomeranian in the sink or basin, be sure to test the temperature of the water on the back of your hand so that it

CHAPTER 10

is not too hot for your dog. Purchase a good-quality dog shampoo and conditioner, not one designed for human hair. After wetting the coat, stroke in the shampoo rather than rub, to avoid creating tangles. Always rinse the shampoo thoroughly out of the coat before applying a conditioner, which should also be well rinsed away.

To clean ears with a cotton swab, you need a very steady hand and a very still dog. A cotton ball or pad is much safer and poses less risk of poking into the ear canal.

You can start by towel-drying the dog and finish with a blow dryer (set on low), concentrating on one area at a time. The head is usually left until last. Many dogs do not like the air blowing into their faces, so please take this into consideration when angling the dryer. Keep your dog in a nice warm place until he is completely dry.

EARS AND EYES

Every dog's ears must be kept clean. To clean your Pom's ears, you may use a cotton pad and a special ear cleaner, usually in liquid or powder form. Always take extreme care not to probe into the ear canal or you could damage the ear.

If your dog has been shaking his head or scratching at his ears, there may well be an infection or an infestation of ear mites. A thick brown discharge and a bad odor are indicative of these problems. Contact the vet right away.

It is also necessary to keep the eyes and areas around them clean. You can use a special formula to clean any tear stains from around the eyes. At any sign of injury to an eye, or if the eye turns blue, veterinary attention must be sought immediately. If an eye injury is dealt with quickly, it can often be repaired; if neglected, it can lead to loss of sight.

NAILS

Nails must always be kept trimmed, but how frequently they need clipping depends very much on the surface upon which your dog walks. Dogs living their lives primarily on carpets or on grass will need more frequent attention to their nails than those who regularly run on hard surfaces like pavement or cement.

Your Pomeranian should be trained to accept nail clipping from an early age. Use nail clippers made for dogs; the "guillotine" type are easy to use. Take great care not to cut the quick, which is the blood vessel that runs through the nail, for this will be painful. It is a good idea to keep a styptic pencil or some styptic powder on hand in case of an accident, as this will stem the blood flow. Cutting just a small sliver of nail at a time is the safest approach.

GROOMING YOUR POMERANIAN

Overview

- Despite what you may think, the Pomeranian's full, abundant coat is actually rather easy to maintain.
- Start the pup out simply with gentle brushing to acquaint him with the grooming routine.
- Your Pom's coat goes through an awkward adolescent stage before reaching full bloom in adulthood.
- The adult coat is brushed and trimmed to achieve the desired rounded appearance.
- Bathing, ear care, eye care and nail trimming are among the other routine grooming tasks.

CHAPTER 11

Pomeranian Puppy Training

Many new owners of Poms ask themselves this question: "Do I really have to train a toy dog?" The advantages of obedience training know no size boundaries. Large dogs and small dogs benefit from a proper canine education. Owners who live with trained dogs are far happier than owners who cope with the daily struggle of living with untrained dogs.

Untrained Poms can be little tyrants! Who wants a whirling ball of fur bossing you around the house, peeing on carpets and

Part of puppy training is determining and teaching the house rules. Will your Pom be allowed on the couch? Whatever you decide, enforce it consistently.

running amok day after day? Not you! Training the Pomeranian presents certain challenges, but the breed fares better in obedience than most of his pint-sized competition in the Toy Group. Poms live to please, and that's a decided advantage when training a dog.

A tiny dog needs a tiny dumbbell, but Poms are capable of all of the same exercises in obedience as his larger counterparts.

Training a puppy of any breed can be challenging. Some take to it like a duck to water, but others present more of a challenge for their owners. Puppy training takes both time and dedication. Consistency is a must.

Always keep in mind that your new Pom puppy is in a completely different environment now. Nothing is familiar to him, so even if training had begun with the breeder, he will realistically have to relearn every-thing. Sounds and smells are unfamiliar, your daily routine is perhaps not quite what he was used to and, very importantly, the door is in a different place!

A dangling cloth looks enticing to puppy teeth, but it's more than just harmless chewing if everything on the table comes tumbling down. Puppy-proof and supervise!

SOCIALIZATION AND EARLY LESSONS

When your Pomeranian first arrives home, begin by getting him used to the immediate members of your family, allowing him time to take stock of his new environment. Instill confidence in him and do not bombard him with too many new faces in his first few days with you. There will be plenty of opportunity to introduce him to your wider circle of friends as the weeks pass.

Depending on the age of your puppy, and whether his course of vaccinations is complete, you may or may not be able to take him out in public places immediately. Whichever the case, I would still advise you to allow him to settle down at home for the first few days before venturing further. There will be lots you can do with your Pomeranian puppy, so you will both undoubtedly have great fun, but please allow him to get sufficient rest, too.

If restricted to your home territory for a little while, you can play games with him, with suitably safe soft toys. Check regularly that sharp or unsafe parts, such as squeakers, do not become detached from the toy. These can cause injury, and your puppy's teeth will be very sharp, so toys can easily be damaged.

Whether or not you plan to show your Pomeranian, it is always good to do a little early training, getting him to stand calmly on a table and to lie on his side to be gently groomed. Both will be helpful on numerous occasions, including visits to the vet, when it is much easier to deal with a well-behaved dog. You will be so proud of your clever companion!

Accustom your puppy to being on a lead, which is always a strange experience for a tiny youngster. Begin by just attaching a simple collar, not too tightly, but it should not fit so loosely that it can be caught on things, causing panic and possible injury. Just put the collar on the pup for a few minutes at a time, lengthening each time period slightly until your puppy feels comfortable in his first item of "clothing." Don't expect miracles; this may take a few days. A word of caution about collars: the Pomeranian's coat grows

Sitting pretty on his own little throne, an untrained Pom will figure out how to rule the kingdom in no time!

quickly, and a collar can become too tight within a few days as the puppy develops. Check that the collar is not too tight around the puppy's neck. If you can fit two fingers between the dog and the collar, that should be sufficient.

When the puppy is comfortable in the collar, attach a small lightweight lead. The one you select must have a secure catch, yet be simple to attach and release as necessary. Until now, your puppy has simply gone where he has pleased and will find it very strange to be attached to someone who is restricting his movements. For this reason, when training my own puppies, I like to allow the pup to "take" me for the first few sessions. I then begin to gently guide him, and soon enough training can start in earnest, with the puppy coming with me as I lead the way. It is usual to begin training the puppy to walk on your left-hand side. When this has been accomplished to your satis-

faction, you can try moving him on your right, but there is absolutely no hurry. If you plan to show your Pomeranian, you will generally move your dog on your left, but there are occasions when it is necessary also to move him on your right so as not to obstruct the judge's view.

As your puppy gets older, you can teach him to sit. Always use a simple one-word command, just "Sit," while exerting gentle pressure on his rump to show him what you expect. This will take a little time, but you will soon succeed; always give plenty of praise when he performs correctly. Never shout or get angry when your dog does not achieve your aim, for this will do more harm than good. If yours is destined to be a show dog, you may decide not to teach him to sit, as he will be expected to stand in the show ring.

When your Pomeranian puppy can venture into public places, begin by taking him somewhere quiet without too many distractions. Soon you will find his confidence increasing, and you can then introduce him to more new places, with exciting sights, sounds and smells. He must always be on a safe lead that cannot be slipped. When you have total confidence in one another, you will probably be able to let him off lead in safely enclosed places like your local dog park. Still it is necessary to keep an eye on him.

CRATE-TRAINING YOUR POMERANIAN

We use the term "crate-training" to mean "house-training," even though the crate has more uses than just teaching the puppy clean indoor habits. Poms are clean dogs, and most Poms pick up house-training quite naturally. If you have been fortunate enough to purchase a puppy from a breeder who introduced the puppy to the crate, then you are ahead of the game. If not, you will introduce

the puppy to his crate on the first day. The crate should be in a room of the house where the family spends a lot of time. Place him in his crate for short intervals throughout his first day. Stay in the room with him.

Don't think of the crate as just a house-training device. It is an all-around safety and comfort tool for your Pom, as he will learn to think of his crate as a special place all his own.

Let him see you. Give him a toy and talk encouragingly to him. After two minutes, let him out and praise him. Repeat this same routine an hour later, but this time make him stay for three or four minutes. By the time evening comes, he won't be afraid of the crate and should be ready for bed.

It's hard to resist the urge to pamper a Pom!

Consistency is your key to house-training. The Pom will not house-train himself. He needs you to be watching him vigilantly day in and day out, at least for the first few months. The crate is helpful because a dog instinctively will not soil his den or sleeping area. Therefore, the crate is the best place for him to sleep overnight and to rest and play when you can't watch him every minute. By spending happy time in the crate, he will learn to love it as his special place.

Puppies always "go" when they wake up, within a few minutes after eating, after play periods and after brief periods of confinement. Remember that every time the puppy is released from his crate, you should take him outside. Stay with him until he relieves himself. Most pups around 12 weeks of age will need to eliminate at least every hour or so, as many as 10 times a day. Always take the puppy outside to the same area, telling him "Outside" as you go out. Use your chosen potty command when he does his business, lavishing praise on him and repeating your key word. Use the same exit door for your potty trips, and, if feasible, the puppy's crate should be in the same room as the exit door so you can get him out quickly. Don't allow him to roam the house until he's house-trained; how will he find that outside door if he's three or four rooms away?

Of course, he will have accidents. All puppies do. You wouldn't expect your toddler to suddenly not need diapers. Potty-training children is actually considerably more difficult than house-training a Pom puppy. Ask any mother changing the diapers of a two-year-old!

When you catch your pup in the act of having an accident, clap your hands loudly, say "Aaah! Aaah!" and scoop him up to go outside. Your voice should startle him and make him stop. Be sure to praise when he finishes his duty outside. He can then rest in his crate while you clean up.

If you discover the piddle spot after the fact…more than three or four seconds later… you're too late. Pups only understand *in the moment*, and will not understand a correction given more than five seconds (that's only *five*) after the deed. Correcting any later will only cause fear and confusion. Just forget it and vow to be more vigilant.

Never rub your puppy's nose in his mistake or strike your puppy or adult dog with your hand, a newspaper or other object to correct him. He will not understand and will only become fearful of the person who is hitting him.

One final, but most important, rule of crate use: never, *ever* use the crate for punishment. Successful crate use depends on your puppy's positive association with his "house." If the crate represents punishment or "bad dog stuff," he will resist using it as his safe place. Sure, you can crate your pup while you clean up after he has sorted through the trash. Just don't do it in an angry fashion or tell him "Bad dog, crate!"

Crates are not only useful in house-training but also necessary for travel. Likewise, in the home, a crate gives your Pom a place to which he can retire with a special bone, out of the way of foot traffic and not underneath you in the kitchen. A Pom puppy is too small to be loose in the house during busy times, like in the morning when the family is trying to get ready for work. Place the Pom in his crate with a toy and know that he's safe.

Show puppies also must learn to use a crate, as a crate is the preferred mode of travel to and from the shows. During the show, the Pomeranian will have to remain safely in his crate when he's not being groomed, trained or exhibited. When you commence crate-training, remain within sight of your dog and give him a toy or something to occupy his mind. Always create a positive association.

To begin with, leave him in the crate for very short spells of just a minute or two, then gradually build up the time span. However, never confine a dog to a crate for long periods. For example, a three-month-old puppy should never be expected to stay in his crate for more than two or three hours at a time. As the puppy's bladder control develops, the length of time can be extended, but never for more than five or six hours at a time (unless overnight when the puppy is sleeping). If you are away at work all day, arrange for a neighbor or dog walker to visit midday.

POMERANIAN PUPPY TRAINING

Overview

- All dogs, of all breeds and mixes, large and small, require obedience training in order to be well behaved.
- The Pom loves to please his owners but, like all puppies, can be challenging for owners to train.
- A well-socialized, confident dog is a better behaved dog. Take your Pom out and about to introduce him to new, positive experiences.
- Basic puppy lessons include introducing pup to his collar and lead and teaching him to behave politely for grooming.
- Crate-training is a reliable way to house-train but offers so many other benefits to dogs and their owners.

POMERANIAN

Basic Commands

The Pomeranian is a lively and intelligent little breed, one that is very capable of learning. However, because of his intelligence, he will probably want to reason things out, so he will need to see *why* you want him to do something. Most Poms will consider the reward of a food treat a perfectly good reason! Consistency in training is of the utmost importance. Of course, you must never be harsh in your training methods. Not only is this cruel, but your Pom will probably rebel—and with good reason.

When teaching commands to your small Pom, it's good to crouch down to get closer to his level. Training won't be much fun with you looming overhead.

All Pomeranians benefit from training, whether pets, show dogs or obedience competitors. In all training, it is essential to get your dog's full attention, which many owners do with the aid of treats, so that the dog learns to associate treats with praise.

Your Pomeranian will likely be curious about the distractions around him, so you will want to have treats handy to bring his attention back to you.

The following training method involves using food treats, although it is possible to wean your dog off these training aids in time, or at least reduce their frequency of use, once the behaviors are learned. As you teach the basic commands, always use very simple commands, just one or two short words, and keep sessions short so that they do not become boring for your dog.

SIT

With the lead in your left hand, hold a small treat in your right, letting your dog smell or lick the treat but not take it. Move it away as you say "Sit," your treat hand rising slowly over the dog's

Looking up at you, focused on the lesson, is how you want your Pom to behave during training sessions.

head so that he looks upward. In looking up to follow the treat, he will bend his knees and sit. When this has been accomplished, give a reward and lavish praise.

If this method fails because your dog backs up instead of

While there's no danger of your Pom's taking *you* for a walk, he still should be taught to heel nicely at your side.

sitting, here's an alternative plan. Place your open left hand behind the Pom's rear end and then place the right hand with the treat in front of his nose. Now lift the treat and the Pom

will back into your palm and sit! *Voila!* Praise him for sitting and repeat the exercise once or twice more.

HEEL

A dog trained to heel will walk alongside his handler without pulling ahead or lagging behind. Again the lead should be held in your left hand while the dog assumes the sit position next to your left leg. Hold the end of the lead in your right hand, but also control it lower down with your left.

Step forward with your right foot, saying the word "Heel." To begin, just take three steps and then command your Pom to sit again. Repeat this procedure until he carries out the task without pulling. Then you can increase the number of strides—five, seven and so on. Give verbal praise at the close of each exercise, and at the end of the training session, let him enjoy himself with a free run.

DOWN

When your dog is proficient in sitting, you can introduce the word "Down." Before beginning, it is essential to understand that a dog will consider the down position as a submissive one, so gentle training is important.

With your Pomeranian sitting by your left leg, as for the sit, hold the lead in your left hand and a treat in your right. For your tiny toy, you will need to crouch down to get close to him. Place your left hand on top of the dog's shoulders (without pushing) and hold the treat under his nose, saying "Down" in a quiet tone of voice. Gradually move the treat along the floor, in front of the dog, all the while talking gently. He will follow the treat, lowering himself down. When his elbows touch the floor, you can release the treat and give praise, but try to get him to remain there for a few seconds before getting up. Gradually, the time of the

down exercise can be increased.

Some trainers advocate teaching the down to a small dog by having the dog sitting on your lap. Hold the treat at the puppy's nose and praise him all the while. Now slowly lower your hand down below your knees. The puppy will follow the food hand and lower his front legs. Now he's in the down position. Praise him. Repeat this a few times, and then try the exercise with him sitting on the sofa next to you.

Teach the down with a combination of verbal commands, hand signals and gentle reassurance.

STAY

Stay can be taught with your dog in either a sit or a down position, as usual with the lead in your left hand and the treat in your right. Allow him to lick the treat as you say "Stay" while standing directly in front of the dog, having moved from your position beside him. Silently count to about five, then move back to your original position alongside him, allowing your Pom to have the treat while you give him lavish praise.

To teach the stay effectively, start out very close to the dog, standing directly in front of him.

Keep practicing the stay just as described above for a few days, then gradually increase the distance between the two of you, using your hand with the palm facing the dog in indication that he must stay. Soon you should be able to do this exercise without a lead (in an enclosed area, of course!), and your Pomeranian will increasingly stay for longer periods of time. Always give lavish praise upon completion of the exercise.

COME

The come exercise presents special challenges to the owner of any spitz breed. These dogs are busy little dogs with full brains and sensitive noses. They would much rather chase the wind than come running back to you. The trick is to convince your Pom that coming back to you will yield wonderful rewards.

Never call your Pom to come and then scold him when he gets to you. *Always* make his coming to you a happy, positive thing. Save your best treats for the come exercise (a piece of cooked chicken, a bit of bologna or a tiny piece of sausage). The idea is to invite him to return, offering a terrific treat and giving lots of praise when he does so. It is important to teach the come command, for this should bring your dog running back to you if ever he is in danger of moving out of sight. It is a command with truly life-saving potential, so you want your dog to *want* to come to you!

Begin practicing the come with your dog on a loose lead. You can encourage him to come to you with a little tug. Once he masters this, you can practice off lead (in a securely fenced area or indoors) from a few feet away. You can increase the distance day by day, and be sure to practice this one every day.

BASIC COMMANDS

Overview

- The Pom is a bright dog, which means that he can be a fast learner, although he may need a little convincing to do things your way.
- Sit is a very basic exercise and the starting point for teaching other commands.
- Every dog should learn to walk politely by his owner's side in the heel position.
- The down should be approached gently as it is a submissive position for dogs.
- Your Pom can be taught to stay by starting out close to you and in short increments, gradually increasing both distance and time.
- The come command is the most important for your dog's safety; it could even save his life!

Home Care for Your Pomeranian

Pomeranians can lead very long and active lives, many going on for 14 years plus, and several have been known to make it even to 20. So, with good care and a little bit of luck, your new Pom friend will be with you for many years to come.

Recognizing signs of the onset of illness is an important factor in keeping your dog healthy and, as you get to know your pet better, you will grow a sort of "sixth sense" as to when he is feeling unwell. Routine care, cleanliness and careful obser-

Your Pom's abundant coat is very inviting to pests that lurk in the tall grass! Get in the habit of checking his coat and skin regularly after time spent outdoors.

vation will help you to see problems arising so that you can take your pet to the vet without delay for further investigation.

DENTAL CARE

Keeping your Pom's teeth in good condition is your responsibility. You owe this to your dog, for dental problems do not just affect the mouth. When gums are infected, all sorts of health problems can subsequently arise, spreading through the system to internal organs and possibly leading even to consequent death. Remember, dental problems are especially prevalent in toy dogs.

Taking extreme care, you should clean the teeth of your Pom very gently indeed, using a tiny toothbrush and special canine toothpaste. Take particular care if any of the teeth are beginning to loosen. Your dog may not like this procedure much at first but should easily get used to it if you

Too bad the Pomeranian can't really brush his own teeth! But this Pom has the right idea...now he just needs his owner's help.

ID tags securely fastened to your Pom's everyday collar are a must every time he leaves the house.

clean regularly. Experienced breeders sometimes use a special dental scraper, but improper use of the scraper can injure the dog and so is not recommended for use by the average pet owner.

When cleaning the teeth, always check the gums for signs of inflammation. If you notice

The puppy fluff can make a collar too tight very quickly, so check your pup's collar daily and adjust it as needed.

that the gums look red or swollen, a visit to your vet would be worthwhile.

RECOGNIZING SYMPTOMS

If you love your Pomeranian and you spend plenty of time together, you will know when something is amiss. He may go off his food or seem dull and listless, and his tail may droop a little. His eyes, usually bright and alive, may seem to have lost their sparkle, and his coat may look dull instead of glistening.

His stool may also be an indication of ill health. Loose stools usually clear up within 24 hours, but if they persist for longer than this, especially if you see blood, you will need to visit your vet. The same rule of thumb applies to constipation and vomiting. Also keep a lookout for increased thirst and/or an increase in frequency of urination, which could indicate a problem.

CHECKING FOR PARASITES

It is essential to keep your dog's coat in first-rate order or parasites may take hold, causing the skin and coat condition to deteriorate. It is often not easy to see parasites, and if you catch sight of even one flea, you can be sure there will be more lurking somewhere. There are several good preventive aids available to protect you dog from external parasites, and your vet will be able to advise you about them. With your Pom's abundant coat, you should frequently check all the way to the skin for evidence of fleas or ticks.

Also be on the continual lookout for ear mites. These pests cannot be seen, but a brown discharge with some odor in the ear is a clear indication that they are present. A suitable ear treatment will be available from your vet.

A dog can also carry internal parasites in the form of worms. Roundworms, hookworms and heartworms are among the most common offenders. Tapeworms, although less frequent, can be very debilitating as well.

Routine worming is essential throughout a dog's life and, again, veterinary recommendation as to a suitable regimen is certainly advised. Fecal exams should be performed and preventives prescribed at your Pom's annual checkups.

HOME CARE FOR YOUR POMERANIAN

Overview

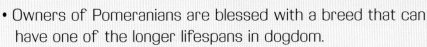

- Owners of Pomeranians are blessed with a breed that can have one of the longer lifespans in dogdom.
- Dental care not only keeps your Pom's teeth clean but also protects him from serious internal disease associated with mouth problems.
- Pay attention to your Pom and any signals that he might be giving you that he is not feeling well.
- Parasites can be pests to all dogs and their owners. Check for signs of internal and external parasites and stay current with your Pom's preventives.

Your Healthy Pomeranian

I t is absolutely important to locate a good veterinarian in your area before you bring your puppy home. The vet will be your Pom's primary healthcare provider, so check with your breeder, your dog-owning friends or the local kennel club for references. It is beneficial to find a vet who has experience with the Pom, or at least toy dogs in general. The vet also should be familiar with the hereditary problems seen in the breed. A good vet will plan your puppy's long-term health care and

The Pom is a sturdy small dog, capable of living well over 14 years with diligent health care. This beauty is Ch. Tarahill Garden Party, owned by Skip Piazza.

help you become dog-smart about canine health issues.

Take your puppy to your veterinarian within three or four days after bringing him home. Show the vet any health records of shots and wormings from your breeder. He will conduct a thorough physical exam to make sure that your Pomeranian pup is in good health and will recommend a schedule for vaccinations, microchipping, routine medications and regular well-puppy visits. A good vet will be gentle and affectionate with a new pup and do everything possible to make sure that the puppy is not frightened or intimidated.

Your veterinarian will manage your Pom's puppy vaccinations as well as the booster-shot program throughout your dog's life.

The importance of dental care as part of your Pom's overall maintenance cannot be overemphasized.

VACCINATIONS

Vaccine protocol for puppies varies with many veterinarians, but most recommend a series of three "combination" shots given at three- to four-week intervals. Your puppy should have had his first shot before he left his breeder. "Combination" shots vary, and a single injection may contain six, seven or even eight vaccines in one shot. Many breeders and veterinarians feel the potency of five or six vaccines in a single shot can negatively compromise a puppy's immature immune system, so they recommend fewer vaccines in one shot or even separating vaccines into individual injections.

The wisest and most conservative course is to administer only one shot in a single visit, rather than two or three shots at the same time, and allow three weeks between shots. That means extra trips to your veterinarian with your puppy and adult dog, but your Pomeranian's healthy immune system is worth your time.

The vaccines recommended by the American Veterinary Medical Association (AVMA) are those that protect against diseases most dangerous to your puppy and adult dog. Called core vaccines, these include distemper, canine parvovirus, canine adenovirus and canine hepatitis. All of these are highly contagious for puppies. They are generally combined into one shot.

Rabies immunization is required in all 50 states, with the rabies vaccine given at least three weeks after the complete series of three puppy shots. However, for many years the rabies vaccine has been available in a one-year and a three-year shot. The obvious wise course would be to vaccinate every third year so as not to administer unnecessary vaccines.

Vaccines no longer routinely recommended by the AVMA, except when the risk is present, are canine parainfluenza, leptospirosis, canine coronavirus, *Bordetella* (kennel cough) and Lyme disease (borreliosis). The author recommends the multi-shot, including leptospirosis, parainfluenza and coronavirus. Although some Pom breeders have reported reactions to the leptospirosis vaccine, we include it as a precaution. Discuss this with your vet before making a decision.

The current AVMA guidelines recommend vaccinating adult dogs every three years instead of annually. Mindful of that, many dog owners now do titer tests to check their dogs' levels of antibodies rather than automatically vaccinating.

Regardless of vaccine frequency, every Pomeranian should visit his veterinarian once a year as an adult and twice yearly as a senior. At the very least, he needs an annual heartworm test before he can receive another year of heartworm preventive medication. Most importantly, the annual visit keeps your vet apprised of your pet's health progress, and the hands-on exam often turns up small abnormalities the lay person can't see or feel.

HEARTWORM

Heartworms are parasitic worms that propagate inside your dog's heart and could ultimately kill your dog. Now

Every dog owner should know how to take her dog's temperature. It's not as bad as it looks!

found in all 50 states, heartworm is delivered through a mosquito bite. Even indoor dogs should take heartworm preventive, which can be given daily or monthly in pill form. Heartworm preventive is a prescription medication available only through your veterinarian. A heartworm test is required before the vet will dispense the medication.

FLEAS AND TICKS

Some folks say that even dinosaurs had fleas! Dogs unfortunately have to contend with these nasty critters. Luckily, today there are various low-toxic, effective preventives—weapons to aid you in your battles with fleas. Discuss them with your vet. Some collars are effective on Poms, but be sure to open the package and expose the collar to the air for a few days before putting it on the dog. Never ignore "a harmless flea," as they can damage a Pom's lovely coat terribly and make him itchy and miserable.

The tick, with its eight strong legs, can burrow into your dog and transmit deadly diseases.

Three tick-borne diseases,

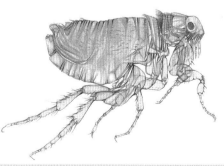

A greatly magnified look at a parasite with which most dogs and owners do battle, the flea.

Lyme disease (canine borreliosis), ehrlichiosis and Rocky Mountain spotted fever, are now found in almost every state and can affect humans as well as dogs. Dogs that live in or visit areas where ticks are present, whether seasonally or

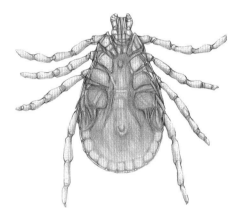

year-round, must be protected.

Ask your veterinarian about spot-on flea and tick treatments as well as insect growth regulators. These products have great track records with dogs. Homespun remedies include brewer's yeast, garlic, citronella and other herbal products, but none has been proven scientifically to be effective.

SUBTLE CHANGES

We've mentioned that your Pom's health is in your hands between his visits to the vet. Be ever-conscious of any changes in his appearance or behavior. Things to consider:

Has your Pomeranian gained a few too many pounds or suddenly lost weight? Are his teeth clean and white or does he need some plaque attackers? Is he urinating more frequently, drinking more water than usual? Does he strain during a bowel movement? Any changes in his appetite? Does he appear short of breath, lethargic, overly tired? Have you noticed limping or any sign of joint stiffness?

These are all signs of serious health problems you should discuss with your vet as soon as they appear. This is especially important for the senior dog, since even minor changes can be a sign of something serious.

It goes without saying that healthy Poms are very happy Poms!

SPAYING/NEUTERING

Spaying/neutering is the best health-insurance policy you can give your Pomeranian. Statistics prove that females spayed before their first heat cycle (estrus) have a 90% less risk of several common female cancers and other serious female health problems. Males neutered before their male hormones kick in, usually before six months of age, enjoy greatly reduced to zero risk of testicular and prostate cancer and other related problems. Neutered males also will be less likely to roam, become aggressive or display those male behaviors that drive most people nuts.

Altering your Pom will not automatically make him fat and lazy, and you need only adjust the dog's diet and increase exercise if weight gain does occur. Statistically, you will make a positive contribution to the pet overpopulation problem and, most importantly, to your dog's long-term health.

YOUR HEALTHY POMERANIAN

Overview

- Choose a vet before your puppy comes home; find a local vet who knows toy dogs. If you don't have a vet, take recommendations from trusted dog people.
- Your vet will pick up where the breeder left off in terms of vaccinations and will manage your Pom's vaccinations for the dog's life.
- Ask your vet to do the appropriate tests and prescribe safe preventives for both internal and external parasites.
- As your Pom's owner and home healthcare provider, you must make your vet aware of any changes that may signal a health problem.
- Spaying and neutering has important health benefits, preventing or reducing the risk of certain cancers and other problems in both sexes.